How To Build a Traveling Ebay Empire on $100

By Randy Coles

D.T. Heel Publications
Knoxville, Tennessee, USA

Copyright © 2016 by D.T. Heel.

All rights reserved.

ISBN-13 : 978-1537542492
ISBN-10 : 1537542494

CONTENTS

Part One : Introduction..5
Part Two : Basics..9
Part Three : The Part About $100.....................15
Part Four : The Part About Traveling..............21
Part Five : Tips and Tricks and Shiz................31
Part Six : Concluding Statements....................41

PART ONE : INTRODUCTION

Most people would be thrilled to have an independent income stream, organically grown out of very little cash investment. They may become less interested when they know they would have to put work into it. It might not be that they don't *want* to work; it's just that they don't necessarily want to spend their time doing this or that particular *kind* of work, exhaustively. Independent income is nice and all, but you would still like to take vacations, right? Who wants to be owned by their creation?

There are also people who merge vacation and work together, or at least they try. Though "vacation" is a lofty word here. *Travel* would be more appropriate. That is to say, not laying on a beach in the sun, but rather moving about and seeing new things. Examples of these kinds of people would be journalists, flight attendants and the near extinct door-to-door salespeople.

The point of this book is to share with you how you can actually do both of these things: build an income stream on a singular, one time investment, while integrating boundless travel into the work, itself. This book is admittedly quite brief, but that is because I would like to explain this to you in very concise terms. With this book, you are not going to get phoney baloney self help garbage disguised as financial advice. Nor will you be reading about blasé business practices that common sense already affords you. This is not snake oil or a referral to another book or blog – this is direct information about concrete steps. You only need apply time and effort.

How do I know anything?

Yeah, how do I? I'm just some guy. Ol' Randy down at the bar. But Ol' Randy has been doing this for over four years now and so far so good. Also, Ol' Randy had a mentor of sorts who had been doing it for over ten years now, full time. Ol' Randy learned a lot and experimented a lot. Ol' Randy doesn't usually talk about himself in the third person this much, though.

The point is that you will see later on where my personal investments and returns are laid out as examples, to the cent. Give or take on the flat percentage assigned to shipping costs (you'll see what I mean later), I believe it's about as solid evidence as a person can have. Solid because I'm not some hotshot wannabe-Fortune 500 CEO talking over your head about finance. I'm just Ol' Randy. Randy Coles. Smiling sunshine down on your babies.

Caution:

For some people, the information in this book is already known if not practiced. When they learned it, however, I presume it was revelatory to them, just as it was to me and just as I intend for it to be for you. But please understand - all I am essentially doing is showing you what is possible with solid numbers behind it. Putting yourself into action and maintaining the universe you create for yourself in doing so – that is all on you. This is not a "get rich quick" book. This is a "let's profit from adventure" book.

In the end, you'll try it or you won't. Of course, if you don't try, then you'll never know, but hopefully these things I explain can make trying simple. If you start small, you can slowly wake up to your full potential.

PART TWO : BASICS

If you already understand how Ebay works, then you can probably skip this part. This section is more or less just a clinical style reference guide for people who have never used Ebay before and want to hit the ground running.

What you need to start
1) Ebay account (www.Ebay.com)
2) Paypal account (www.paypal.com)
3) Postal scales (available for sale on Ebay)
4) Shipping material (for fabrics, use gray polymer bags, also for sale on Ebay)
5) Scotch / packing tape
6) A bank account
7) A digital camera
8) Measuring tape
9) Printer with paper or labels

Additionally, these items would be helpful
1) Ebay app for mobile phone
2) Excel or another spreadsheet program

Before you get started
1) Associate your Paypal account with your Ebay account **(Ebay.com -> Account -> personal information, under "financial information")**

2) Associate your bank account with your Paypal account **(paypal.com -> Tools -> Business setup -> account setup)**

How to list

1) Purchase the item that you would like to sell.
2) Take pictures of the item
3) On Ebay.com, click "Sell" at the top
4) Enter the name of the item and all major details you can fit in the box under "Tell us what you're selling" and click "Get Started."
5) Select the correct category for your item. Ebay will guess this automatically, but sometimes you need to change it.
6) Upload photos of your item. Be sure to include photos of any damage to the item.
7) Enter the item specifics in the drop down menus. You can select from what is populated by Ebay or type your own.
8) Enter everything you know about the item in the "Details" box. Be sure to include:
    a. Size / dimensions / measurements
    b. Physical description
    c. Brand
    d. Unique attributes
    e. Any damage or flaws
9) Select the listing format (Auction or Fixed Price) and enter the price (or opening bid for an auction.

10) Choose whether or not you allow for buyers to make you an offer on the item.
11) Select the quantity of items that you have
12) Select your Listing Duration, or how long the items will be on sale.
13) Weigh your item. Add a few grams for packaging and round up to the next ounce.
14) Choose the shipping services you will use.
15) Make sure your associated Paypal email address is correct, along with your zip code, handling time, and whether or not you take returns for the item.
16) Click "List it."

How to ship, once your item has sold

1) Go to Ebay.com and click "My Ebay" up top on the right. From the drop down, select "Selling."
2) Scroll down to your "Sold" items and click the 5th option under that, "Awaiting Shipment." This will limit your view to only items that still need to be sent out.
3) Place your item in a polymer bag (or whatever you want to ship it in) and tape it up securely.
4) Weigh your item and round up to the nearest ounce.
5) Locate the item on you Ebay Sold list and click "Print Shipping Label" out to the right.
6) Select the correct weight and shipping service in the middle column.
7) Click "Purchase postage" in the right column.

8) On the next screen, click "Print label" and then print the shipping label.
9) Tape / glue the label on to your package.
10) Drop the package off at the post office.

Selling limits:

Typically, Ebay starts you off only able to list 10 items. As you approach that maximum number, they will increase your amount. (You can also call them and request this.) Depending on what level of store subscription you purchase, you will have a set number of free listings per month. This includes items that automatically relist themselves and you will have to pay a small fee to list any items that exceed your amount of free listings. I suggest starting small and building up. For example, once you use your first free listings, then you will want to purchase the smallest subscription, which is taken out of your sales. Once you outgrow the smallest package, move to the next one and so on.

Returns:

You will definitely sell more if you accept returns. The downside is that you have to deal with all sorts of people who want to return things for dumb reasons and occasionally give you hell and try to scam you. The bottom line is that you really need to make sure your description of the item being sold is 100% accurate. If there is damage, or if the item looks old and beat up, be sure to mention that in the description. This is because:

1) If a buyer returns the item due to not being accurately described, you will have to pay the return shipping and also refund them the shipping they initially paid.
2) If a buyer returns the item due to it not fitting or simple buyer's remorse, they will have to pay the return shipping and you do not have to refund them the shipping they initially paid.

Organization:

It is best to keep all your items listed on a spreadsheet as you build your inventory. If you note the price you paid for each item, it is easier to see whether or not a best offer is worth it. You will also want to note a location for where you keep the item as your inventory grows. It is also extremely helpful to upload your spreadsheet to your phone (along with the Ebay app). This will allow you to accept best offers from anywhere, and also compare them to the information on your spreadsheet. It is usually best to accept best offers as soon as they come in. And if the offer is too low, always counteroffer.

Caution:

The best way to grow the business is to accept loss when it happens, stay patient, and keep your ego out if it. You will have occasional buyers acting unreasonable and annoying. You will have to issue refunds sometimes that will lose you money. You will make mistakes and you will wonder if some items are never going to sell. You have to keep moving ahead. Losing a few dollars here and there does not matter if you have a greater amount of money coming in. If someone is actively attempting to extort you or rip you off, you can call Ebay about it and they can assist you in working it out. Don't let yourself get walked on, but unfortunately, the customer is usually right…even if they are not. It can be frustrating to watch an item sit for months and not sell, but if you focus on what is selling, you will see that you will always come out ahead in time.

PART THREE : THE PART ABOUT THE $100

Okay! Do you have your crisp $100 bill? Great! What you need to do is to go down to your local thrift store and spend every penny of it. Maybe make a day of it between several thrift stores. Either way, buy what calls out to you. Be it clothing (a very practical jumping off point), board games, VHS tapes, books or children's toys; buy the things that feel familiar to you. If they speak to you, they will speak to other potential buyers. (Unless you are a complete freak, but then again, you weren't the one who put it on the rack!)

Alright now. You bought all this stuff and brought it back at your house. Sort it out and take photographs of it. Follow the instructions in The Basics to get all of it accurately inspected and listed for sale on Ebay. Naturally, you will want to mark your items up for at least double what you paid for them, though in most cases you can usually sell for much higher than double. And if you are using the Ebay's "Best Offer" option, then you have nothing to lose with a higher price. You can also see how much an item is selling for by looking it up and viewing "Sold items only."

Got your items listed? Good. Now wait. And yes, waiting hurts when you first begin, but this is part of it. Of course, you could always be making more investments to grow it quicker if you *did* have more than

$100 to spare, but in a worse case scenario, you need only spend $100 and then you wait. It may take over a month to make a single sale or receive any offers. Items may be listed and relisted again. Some items may *never* sell. But if you wait, eventually, you will make your money back and then some.

So let's say you did! You did make some money back! Let's say you spent $100 and purchased 50 items at two dollars apiece. Then let's lowball here and say you sold just 20 items at seven dollars apiece. Well that is $140 you earned and you still have 30 items left to sell. Ebay and Paypal fees combined are about an average of 12%, depending on what you sell. Let's roll with that against the $140 you have, leaving you with $125 and 30 items left in your inventory.

You made your hundred dollars back, and also $25 extra. Now you have options: Either go back to a thrift store and spend the entire $125, or just spend another $100 and keep $25 for yourself or your business. If you purchase 50 more items as before, then you'll have 80 items in your inventory to generate more money. See the cycle of perpetuity here?

Additional considerations:

First of all, if you believe in what you are trying to do here, then you may as well just list each item with duration of "Good-til-cancelled." The more inventory you have, the more visible all your other items will become. As long as you are always adding inventory, and not subtracting, your business will continue to grow.

The $100 figure is not a rule. The same cycle of cash flow can be achieved with $10, $100, $2043, whatever. It's proportional to time, though. Basically, the less you spend, the longer you will likely have to wait to make it back.

Think of it this way: the thrift store was going to sell it anyway, if not to you, then someone else. You are working as a facilitator, buying it at the lowest price and then reselling for what the item is actually worth. The true value of an item is something that thrift stores rarely know or care about. They are more about facilitation and processing, not mining for gold, or even a lesser metal. That is your job: to extract quality from the quantity, present it nicely, and find it a good home.

Real world application:

My very first run of this kind was at a thrift store in Indianapolis. I spent $96.82 on a total of 33 items. Three years to the day, it had all been sold except one item, and I had earned $356.94. After taking out the 12% for Ebay and PayPal, that left $318.69. Those figures also included shipping, which I will also very liberally assign another 12% for (actual shipping was too far across time for me to gather hard numbers on the actual percentage, but 12% represents a heavier than usual average shipping weight for good measure). That leaves $284.55 earned over time, almost tripling my initial investment. And though this reflects a period of three years, my initial investment alone was earned back much sooner.

As I got more comfortable and knowledgeable of it, I spent more and priced higher. One year later I visited two different thrift stores in Asheville, North Carolina. Between the two, I spent $423.75 on a total of 118 items. Two years later, 82 items had been sold, having earned me $1150.76. The fees and shipping knocked my take down to $917.37, which still more than doubled my money while leaving 36 items from that haul still in my inventory.

Shall we jump ahead one more year for a clearer picture? It was another run to Asheville and I had spent $375.24 on a total of 117 items. Just *one* year later, 82 items had been sold, and $1306.55 had been earned. Take out for fees and shipping and I was left with

$1041.57 and still 35 items left over. And yes…it took two years to sell 82 items the first time and just one year to sell the same number, the second time. The speed of return literally doubled from one year to the next because the longer you do it and the more you spend, the quicker the money comes.

Tripling your money in three years, or doubling it in one or two, is still more lucrative then anything your bank would do with it. Why settle for a 1.5% return on a certificate of deposit when you can earn back over 100% in a similar amount of time by investing in tangible goods?

PART FOUR : THE PART ABOUT TRAVELING

Different cities have different thrift stores, and also different cultural norms that dictate what types of items can be found in those stores. A person could always resell strictly from the places they know locally, but he or she would not be diversifying their inventory outside the tastes of a single city. This can lead to stagnation in your inventory. So first things first, if you expand your purchasing out to other cities, it can only help your business to grow.

Think about sports, for example. If you live in Pittsburgh, you can find licensed Steelers clothing in almost any thrift store in town. It's the local team, so naturally the local brand is moved around more frequently among its citizens. You can spend all of your days buying up Pittsburgh jerseys and turning them around for a profit, sure, but not everyone is a Steelers fan. Some people like the Saints and you could earn more by diversifying your line of inventory out to that team as well. So where would you find a bunch of inexpensive Saints jerseys? New Orleans, of course! And there is your reason to travel there. On the way, you can pick up even more teams in more cities. (Kentucky Wildcats and the Tennessee Volunteers college football merchandise tend to sell well.)

Of course, there are other considerations, such as lodging and gas. So I'm sure your next question is, all things considered, can I actually *profit* from a trip like that? The short answer is: absolutely.

Before you begin:

Be sure you have already mastered the prior two parts of this book before you dive too deep into this one. If your budget only ever remains at $100, then you can't expect traveling to be very fruitful for you. This section is for sellers who are willing to throw larger amounts of money on the line and are more interested in the travel aspect, then simply earning income with little investment.

Short trips:

If this is something you want to put into practice, it's best to start with short trips as a means of putting your toes in the water. They may last a day or a weekend and can be easily built around other commitments. You may want to research different thrift stores in different cities and make your choice based on special sales on certain days. Or perhaps you choose your city because there is a friend there you would like to visit, or a band you would like to see perform.

It matters not why you ultimately choose where you travel to, but that you spend a portion of your time browsing through racks and making purchases. If you have done this with the intention of reselling, then consider what is a tax write off here: the inventory, the gas, the car rental (if you rented a car), your meals, your lodging (if you stayed overnight), and any other necessities you may be responsible for to make the trip happen. But taxes aside, can you actually make the money back from all those expenses? Yes and you can profit.

Daytrips are a day's work or less. What is the nearest major city? Go there and spend two hours filling up a cart. Use discretion, but less than what is described in Part Three. That is to say, do not purchase simply what calls to you, but also what reminds you of others. Perhaps you have no connection to a pretty pink Rainbow Brite t-shirt at all, but surely you know someone else would, right? Throw it in the cart! And keep throwing things in the cart until the cart is overfull. Thank your clerk for his or her patience (though usually they are happy to work with one person who is expected to take a long time, as it can be a step back from hustle and bustle of an otherwise busy store), and load everything into your car. Eat a good meal, drive home, sleep on it and start listing the next day. If you put it all on Ebay, in a few months, you will have made back all that you spent on inventory, your gas money and your meal. Easy peasy.

Maybe you would rather make a weekend of it. Why not go to Lexington, Kentucky in May and take in the horse races after you load up at one of their excellent second-hand stores? (Where do you think all their fancy clothes go after the racing season?) After the races, have a meal and get a room – or save money and pitch a tent – or save more money and sleep in your car. The next day you can head north through the Ohio Valley where their Goodwill stores are entirely half price every Saturday.

Load up at all of them, eat well in Cincinnati and then drive home. As with a daytrip, list it on Ebay and, in time, it will all have been paid for (except for your gambling debts, naturally).

Long trips:

If you can turn a profit on a short excursion, then you can turn a profit on a long one. It's actually all just relative to the amount of inventory you purchase. Long trips, however, take more planning because you will have to figure out two main things: how much will you have to buy in order to cover your costs and how will you transport it back to your home or office?

There really is no limit to the number of stops you can make in order to grow your business. Every place you mine is just more money in the bank eventually, as long as you can get the inventory back to your home base. So much depends on the distance you are driving and how long you will be gone. For tax purposes, you can only write off investments on the way to each destination, so a good rule of thumb is to make your thrift runs at least on each leg of the trip (and certainly in larger metropolitan or particularly wealthy areas). But keep in mind that if you are driving from Las Vegas to Albuquerque and you detour down to Phoenix but never make a thrift run, then you can't rightly write that off as business. So if you want to go to Phoenix, you need to visit their thrift shop or else you have disrupted the balance of work and pleasure.

As for transport, a longer time on the road means more space gets taken up in your vehicle as you go. The number of people coming along also makes a difference so you probably should not travel with more than one other person, lest your precious space be taken by the luggage of a third wheel. It would not hurt to own a hatchback vehicle. Usually, a midsize SUV is decent enough for a long journey, but it will fill up as any vehicle will. I know one fellow who hauls a trailer and keeps his inventory in there, using the collapsed seat and trunk of his sedan as a bed. You also always have the option of renting a vehicle, though that will also cut into your costs. If you do this, check with your insurance company to see if you even need to purchase renter's insurance or if they cover you fully. If you have no transferable coverage than call a third party company to insure your vehicle, rather than the rental company, and you will save a lot of money.

You want to pack as light as you can for to save space for your inventory, and also spend as little as possible on accommodations. Though hotel stays are sometimes inevitable, camping is, by far, the most inexpensive way to lodge for an evening. Pitching a tent sounds like a pain, but a $60 pop up tent can set up in two seconds and break down in two minutes, while taking up very little space in your vehicle. Perhaps rustic camping is not to one's liking, but the variety of KOA grounds across North America generally have full facilities and cost an average of about $30 per night, sometimes more or less, depending on where you are.

Many state and provincial parks also have camping, less costly than that, and also with full facilities.

There are many more costs associated with a longer trip than a shorter one, no matter how you cut the cake. So if you buy a small amount of inventory, it will take longer to make your money back. Again, the longer the trip, the more spending on inventory you should do. However, if you are dedicated to making these journeys continuously, you will find that where you may experience loss on a large journey, it will be more than covered by any number of smaller excursions before or after. Or, if you prefer: it all works out in the end.

Real world application:

My home base is in Tennessee, of course, because that's where people like me are from. But I do have some family up in Pittsburgh, and some very good friends in Baltimore. Exactly eleven months prior to me sitting here typing this now, I drove up there, hit up the thrift stores in Pittsburgh and then spent time with my grandmother. Then I moved on to Frederick, Maryland, where I met with my friends from Baltimore, got a hotel, visited my favorite brewery and ate some really good food. The next morning, I woke up and went directly out to the Frederick thrift shops. After a few hours of mining, I loaded it all in and drove to Baltimore where I rejoined with my friends at their home. I had a good time and they had a spare bedroom. The next morning, I checked out some Batlimore thrift spots on my way out of town.

That entire journey covered five days and I purchased $736.40 in new inventory. Lodging only cost me two nights, the hotel in Frederick and also a campsite late night before I made it into Pittsburgh - but that was fluke due to a late start because I made a last minute decision to purchase new tires for my car. I'll count it, though, since not everyone reading this has grandmothers and friends. Total for lodging was about $95. Gas ran me about six tanks at an average of about $25 per tank, so around $150 for that. Food ended up being about $75, all in all. So my total expenses for the journey were just slightly over $1000 and I had brought back 203 new items with me.

So how did it turn out? Well, I like I said, it has not quite been a year yet at the time of this writing, but I have sold 102 items, just over half, and earned a total of $1542.93. After fees and shipping, that comes down to $1230.01. That means that in less than a year, I have earned not quite double the amount I spent on inventory, also covered all of my lodging, meals and gas, and still banked over $200 with more to come. It's like getting paid to visit your family and friends!

Earlier that same year, I decided to give a go at an extensively long trip to see how it would work out. I rented a mid-size SUV and spent about fifteen days and six thousand miles on the longest drive I had ever taken. I headed first north to Kansas City, where I squandered the opportunity to thrift under the false I idea that I would "fill up too much space too soon." (You can always ship inventory back to yourself – there is no "filling up too much space too soon.") I continued west across South Dakota, Wyoming, Idaho, Montana and Washington, all the way to Seattle. It was not until I was that far that I made my first actual thrift visit. A buddy who knew I was coming to town met me there unannounced, making me feel rushed and impolite and so I cut that one far shorter than it should have been. (I found some great stuff in the time I had, though.) I only spent $65.71 on 29 items. After Seattle, I stayed with more friends in Portland and, again, squandered another opportunity to visit thrift stores there – in Portland of all places. Shame on me, I know. Next up was downtown San Francisco, which was an utter nightmare. Everything was overpriced, parking was impossible, there were no shopping carts and the sense of style was bland. (Thanks, Silicone Valley!) I spent 119.18 on just 32 items, many of them t-shirts representing tech companies. The trip had been amazing, but my thrift picking was off to a very lean start.

    Los Angeles was a breath of fresh air with some really likable people running the thrift shops down along Wilshire Blvd. All in one store, I spent $315.65 and purchased 75 items. Some things were pricier, which was to be expected on the west coast, but the quality was fantastic and more expensive items were offset by plenty of cheaper ones. From there, it was out across the desert to Las Vegas, which is comparable to the South Eastern United States as a second hand Mecca. There I got the most bang for my buck, spending $382.61 on 139 items. After that I made the long drive home.

That makes the total spent on inventory for the whole trip $883.15 and my inventory added 275 items.

Now, this trip was experimental and I did not intend to necessarily pay the entire thing off in a single venture. Yet still, I also did not intend to come home with so few items and so many missed opportunities. So in a lot of ways, I flubbed it beyond what I would normally consider reasonable. Then there were the additional costs, such as a $146 parking ticket in LA, the $560 car rental, gas in Death Valley, or breathing and moving in San Francisco. All of these things, plus gas, food, lodging and tolls, ran me right around $2600 in total for the entire trip. Add the cost of my inventory to that and it comes out to right around $3500 spent, there and back.

So one year and three months later, did I make it all back? No. But will I? Probably. At the time of writing this, I had sold 174 of the items purchased and earned $2465.84 from them. Taking out for fees and shipping, using the two averages of 12% each, brings the total take down to $1965.75. That means that I still have 101 items from that trip left in my inventory and have more than doubled my earnings against what I spent. Perhaps in another eight months, the entire cost of the trip will have been paid away. But for now, all of it has been covered, but for $1500, give or take. Fifteen hundred dollars to square the continental United States on your own pace and schedule is otherwise unheard of. And of course, that remaining amount will only be further offset as the future persists and remaining inventory continues to sell.

PART FIVE : TIPS AND TRICKS AND SHIZ

These are some things I've learned that may be useful to you. I already mentioned some of it here and there in the previous sections, depending on how pertinent they were to the context. This is just a grouping of practical information that may save you some time and hassle as you go.

Ebay:
Price high and allow buyers to make offers.

As your inventory grows, always run a sale on *something*. This will increase your traffic, as well as your sales.

Never remove listings because they are not selling. "Good-til-cancelled" is the duration that will be the less maintenance for you. Change the wording in the title or lower the price if an apparent stagnation is intolerable to you.

Be extremely detailed, but concise in your item descriptions. Be sure to list the measured dimensions of the item, and any damage or wear that it has incurred. If there is pertinent information that you simply do not know, then state that you do not know it. Take pictures of every detail, including damage and wear.

Start small and build. Ebay is programmed to help you in this fashion. When the time comes to move up to paying a subscription fee for a store, then do not hesitate.

Take returns and be fair with everyone. Let small things go, even if they are financial. A good reputation and positive feedback are worth the cost. However...

Don't take guff from hucksters. If you are selling something expensive, take photos right before you ship, charge a restocking fee, and fight to the bitter end if they try to return something *they* damaged or if they claim the item was misrepresented when you know it was not. It may seem like a losing battle, going through appeals, and the buyer may leave negative feedback. But the moment you send them a refund, you accept defeat. If there is larger money on the line, and you can prove you are right, fight it to the end. Ebay may eventually refund them out of your money at first, but if you have the proof, then you have an appeal. Ebay will eventually refund you out of their bank and also remove the negative feedback.

When trying to make appeals on the phone, not all Ebay employees will understand. If you reach one does not, thank them for their time, politely say goodbye, and go do something else for a while. Then call back again and talk to someone else about it.

Remember that sometimes you will still lose money, either way. Mistakes happen. Learning is an imperfect experience or else it would be a pointless one. Keep in mind that, all things considered, when you look at your income for a week or a month or a year, that loss is a drop in the bucket against your river of gains. Keep swimming.

Thrift stores:

Different stores and different cities have different sales and discounts at different times. There are some that price everything half off every Saturday, or sometimes just the first Saturday of every month, or perhaps for ten days at the end of the year. When you know what stores have what sales when, it makes for more efficient timing to your travels.

Different stores in different cities also have different reward programs. Sign up for every one that you can. Even if you doubt you will ever be in that city again, it is still better to have the card for two reasons: First, if the store is large enough to issue a rewards card, then the card most likely represents an entire district, which contains many stores and cities. So if you don't plan on returning to that city, what about the city a little further up the road? Secondly, a lot of times, your card only offers a discount after the first visit. Better safe than sorry.

Bags are also a thing at some stores. Sometimes you will get a discount for bringing your own bags, and sometimes (at least in the northwestern USA) you will incur a small charge if you *don't* bring your own bags. Then there are other stores that actually give you a discount for bringing bags to them for later use. (So hang on to your old bags for those types, found mostly in the southeastern USA.)

Be confident in your purchases. Remember that you are only looking for something that someone *else* would want to own. The thrift shop already vetted that item for you or else it would not have made it to the selling floor. If they think someone would buy it, and you also think someone would buy it, then most likely, someone would buy it.

Your best practice as a picker is to start at one rack or shelf and canvass the entire thing, item by item. Even though others around you will usually notice what you are doing and resist interfering, there are some who are dead set to dive in to the center of your path. *Keep going.* Get as close to them as you need to be and, nine times out of ten, they will lose that game of chicken because you were there first and your mission is all business. On the rare occasion that some person wants to continue their obstruction, just say, "let's switch" and jump them. They will awkwardly move down and probably exit the area in two minutes or less.

If you have a full cart, most other customers will not take up the line behind you, instead electing to go to a register that moves more quickly. If you do have someone get behind you and complain, then just ignore that person or direct her to another lane. I only use the female pronoun because this actually happened to me once, where a woman started loudly complaining on her phone that she was going to be "stuck there a while" because she was behind me. She was even insistent on helping me unload my cart to "move it along," while two other lanes were whizzing people through. She eventually took her hands out of my cart and got in another lane - like she should have done ten minutes earlier. Be professional and let people like that sort out adulthood for themselves. You owe no one an apology for buying lots of stuff. They are only embarrassing themselves.

On the other side of the register, it is rare to find a clerk who is displeased to be waiting on a customer who is making a large purchase. If they care at all about the store's financial standing, then they are pleased to see your money being spent there. Elsewise, a lot of them enjoy the break from a hard and constant workflow. When they are dealing with one person, purchasing so much, both parties tend to take it as granted that the check out process is going to take a little bit of time. The stress of customers waiting in their line is often vanquished, as mentioned above. Also, your long receipt and abnormally high dollar amount will tend to be novel to you both. I have had some really pleasant connections with thrift shop clerks. There are some that I encounter on a semi-regular basis and the feelings are warm.

Organization:

Keep a simple spreadsheet that lists all the items in your inventory, the price you paid for them, and where they are located. You can also add columns for what you sell the items for, dates of purchase and anything else that may be useful to you. You can reference it when considering offers.

Depending on what you are selling, plastic bins or shelves tend to make for good methods of storage, but as your inventory grows, understand that you have to know exactly where to find it. Organization by date of purchase seems to work best, so long as you keep up with it on a spreadsheet as mentioned above.

As your inventory leaves, you will have to condense down that which remains. Essentially, this is the same concept as "rotating stock." If an item goes two years without selling, I move it to a bin marked with the year of purchase and aggressively discount and auction it until it is gone. Anything left over after a year of that will be bundled together and sold as a lot.

Be sure to have a decent looking space to photograph your inventory. A blank wall is usually fine, or you can hang up a sheet or something if you have stickers and writing all over your walls.

Keep shipping supplies on hand, as well as a space to do your packaging.

A thermal label printer is also far more resourceful and quick than a standard desktop printer. You can buy them for less than $70 these days on Ebay and elsewhere.

PROTIP: The thermal printer labels are pricier if you buy the industry standards with attached plastic spools. So instead, carefully break the spool that came with your first roll so that you can remove and replace the labels easily. Then you can just buy the rolls in bulk and reuse the same spool. (Randy Coles is not to blame if you mess this part up, but it's really no big loss if you do.)

Also, don't forget to hang on to your receipts, especially if you have filed a business charter and intend to operate as such. You'll need those come tax time.

The Road:
A smart phone is obviously invaluable in so many ways. You can use it to locate thrift stores, of course, but also to keep up with your inventory spreadsheets and handle Ebay offers from the road.

Traveling alone can be a beautiful experience, but so can traveling with one other person. Anymore than that and you'll find it difficult to handle your business, with less space to handle it in.

Keep a canister of mace within arms reach while in your vehicle or your tent. I have never had to use mine, but you never know.

All across North America, it's generally not a problem to pull into a campground after hours and pay in the morning. A lot of places even have night registration drop boxes. Northern Illinois is a hard exception, however, and others may also exist in places I don't know about.

You can get a good pop-up tent for about $60 and they make camping insanely simple. You literally unzip them and throw them into the air and, like sorcery; a tent falls to the ground. Throw in a pillow and sleeping bag, close your eyes and sleep. Or if you're feeling froggy, add a lantern and read a book.

If you are not the camping type, or the weather is awful, keep in mind that the cheapest hotels are not as advertised as major chains. The most inexpensive hotels I have ever stayed in were all located simply by driving by. Sometimes you have to wake the owner up to check in, but they are always pleased to have the business. Also at these types of places, the décor is typically rather outdated, but that tends to be part of the charm for me (with particular consideration to the awesome, retro motor lodges along the Trans Canadian Highway). If you feel weird about any of it, just use your own sleeping bag and pillow on top of the bed comforter.

FUN FACT: In Tennessee, there is no open container law against one beer and two people in a car, even when in motion!

PART SIX : CONCLUDING STATEMENTS

The great Deepak Chopra said something about how the things that progress in our lives are those to which we give our attention and intention. This is no different. You can list ten new items a day and keep buying more and more and selling more and more and really flourish. Or you can go easy and make a few extra hundred dollars per month with a relaxed hand. The choice is yours and the fact you have that choice is a really beautiful aspect of this work, along with the technology and human behavior that allow it.

The best advice is the simplest. Test the waters and take it slow at first. The more you grow this new aspect of your universe, the more you will be able to rely on it for steadier income. Be patient, confident and determined and you will progress to the level of your choice.

Also remember that Ebay need only even be a stepping-stone. Whether full on or casually engaged, you will learn new things that will lead to new epiphanies. These epiphanies will open new doors to new experiences and new ways to make money. But as far as jumping off points go; this is a good one.

Another nuance worth mentioning is that you will also come to find items that speak so much to you, that you will simply have to keep them for yourself. And so consider specializing your sales in a type of product that you personally desire. For example, if you are a person who wishes to exemplify ones identity through footwear, then consider going to the thrift store and purchasing every pair of shoes that you are slightly curious about. You can take them all home and try them on; keep what you want and profit from the rest. Maybe it's not shoes. Maybe it's evening gowns, or beer t-shirts, video games or books. Use this work to enhance your personal style or collection.

Above all, though, keep in mind that you are undertaking an *experience*. Yes, you will make money. Yes, you will find cool stuff to call your own. Beyond all that, though, you are filling your eyes with new horizons, and transience is among the greatest of all therapies. With this guide, I want you to feel confident in the notion of expansion. Furthermore, I want you to feel financially *safe* when making decisions to visit new lands. I want you to know that if you just put a little bit of money into the local community that you find yourself in, you can cover the cost it took to get you there and have a little left over for yourself.

I cannot emphasize enough, that you get what you give. The more time and money you spend, the faster the gears will spin and the larger your return on investment will be. Stay diligent and open on your search and you are almost certain to discover hidden treasure, as well as the people who wish to purchase it.

I love you.
        –Randy Coles

www.ingramcontent.com/pod-product-compliance
Lightning Source LLC
Chambersburg PA
CBHW030704190526
45164CB00004B/414